What's washed up on Shore?

Contents

1 What's washed up on shore?	2
2 Ships and bottles	4
3 Sea creatures	8
4 Toys	12
5 Plastic waste	16
Glossary	20
Index	21
What washed up?	22

Written by Ben Hubbard

Collins

1 What's washed up on shore?

In the 1980s, strange orange objects washed up on a beach in Brittany, France. They were telephones shaped like a well-known cartoon cat.

Hundreds more telephones washed up over the next 30 years. Nobody knew where they had come from. Then, in 2019, the mystery was solved. Some people found a **shipping container**, which had fallen off a ship and washed up in a cave. It was full of more of the same telephones!

Millions of objects appear on shores around the world every year. Some are small, some are big and many are strange. Let's find out more about what has washed up.

2 Ships and bottles

Shipwrecks are ships that sink or become stranded. Some shipwrecks wash up on shore. Many ships have been wrecked on the 'Skeleton Coast' in Namibia, Africa. The water here is rough and dangerous and the winds are strong.

In 1945, the *Otavi* ship got lost in fog near the Skeleton Coast. After a while, it became wrecked on the shore. The crew survived, but the *Otavi* stayed stuck in the sand and is still there now.

In 2018, Tonya Illman found a bottle on Wedge Island beach, Australia. Inside was a handwritten message from the captain of the *Paula* ship. He had thrown the bottle overboard into the Indian Ocean in 1886 and wanted to see where the bottle would land. The message gave the ship's details and asked for it to be returned to the captain.

The bottle drifted for thousands of miles before reaching Australia 132 years later. It is the oldest message in a bottle ever found.

The *Paula*

The rolled-up scroll revealed the captain's message.

3 Sea creatures

In 2024, 40 **pilot whales** became stranded on a beach in Northland, New Zealand.

The whales could not swim back out to sea and would die if they dried out.

Hundreds of people arrived to help the whales. They poured water over their skin and lifted them onto sheets. When the tide came in, the people refloated the whales out to sea.

On Christmas Day in 2022, nine-year-old Molly Sampson made an amazing discovery on a beach in Maryland, USA.

It was a tooth belonging to the largest shark in the world: megalodon.

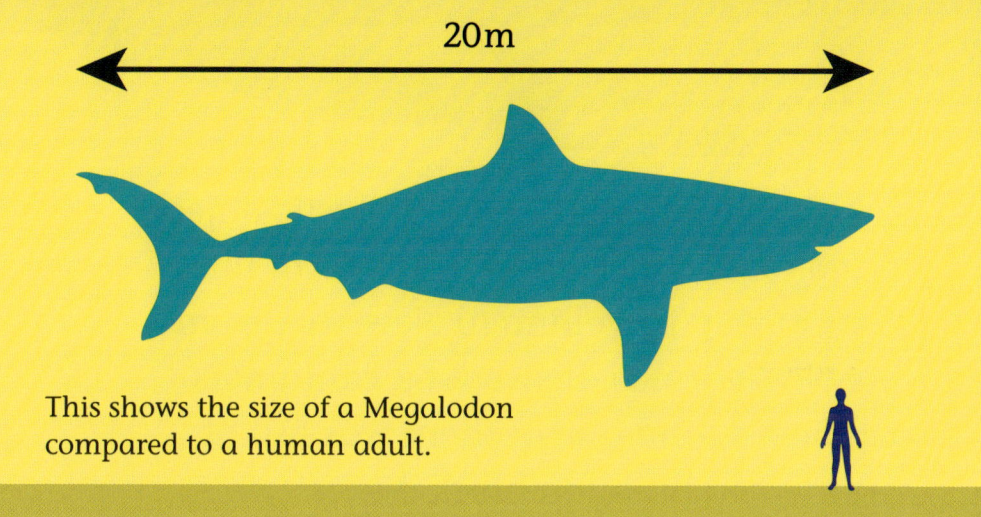

This shows the size of a Megalodon compared to a human adult.

The tooth was nearly 13 cm long and as big as Molly's hand. Luckily, megalodon died out around 3.5 million years ago.

This is what the Megalodon might have looked like.

4 Toys

Cat phones are not the only plastic objects found on beaches. In 1997, a storm hit a cargo ship travelling to New York from The Netherlands. It swept 62 containers overboard, and one of them was full of sea-themed building block pieces.

The pieces have been washing up on Britain's coasts ever since. Some pieces have become collector's items, such as the black octopus.

The container held 4,756,940 building block pieces, including scuba tanks, light grey sharks and black octopuses.

Shipping containers like this are used around the world.

Shipping containers are often lost at sea. In 1992, twelve containers slipped off a ship near Hong Kong. The containers spilled 28,000 plastic toys into the water.

The toys included yellow ducks, red beavers, blue turtles and green frogs.

After a few months, the plastic toys began washing up on shores around the world.

This map shows the toys' journey and where they landed.

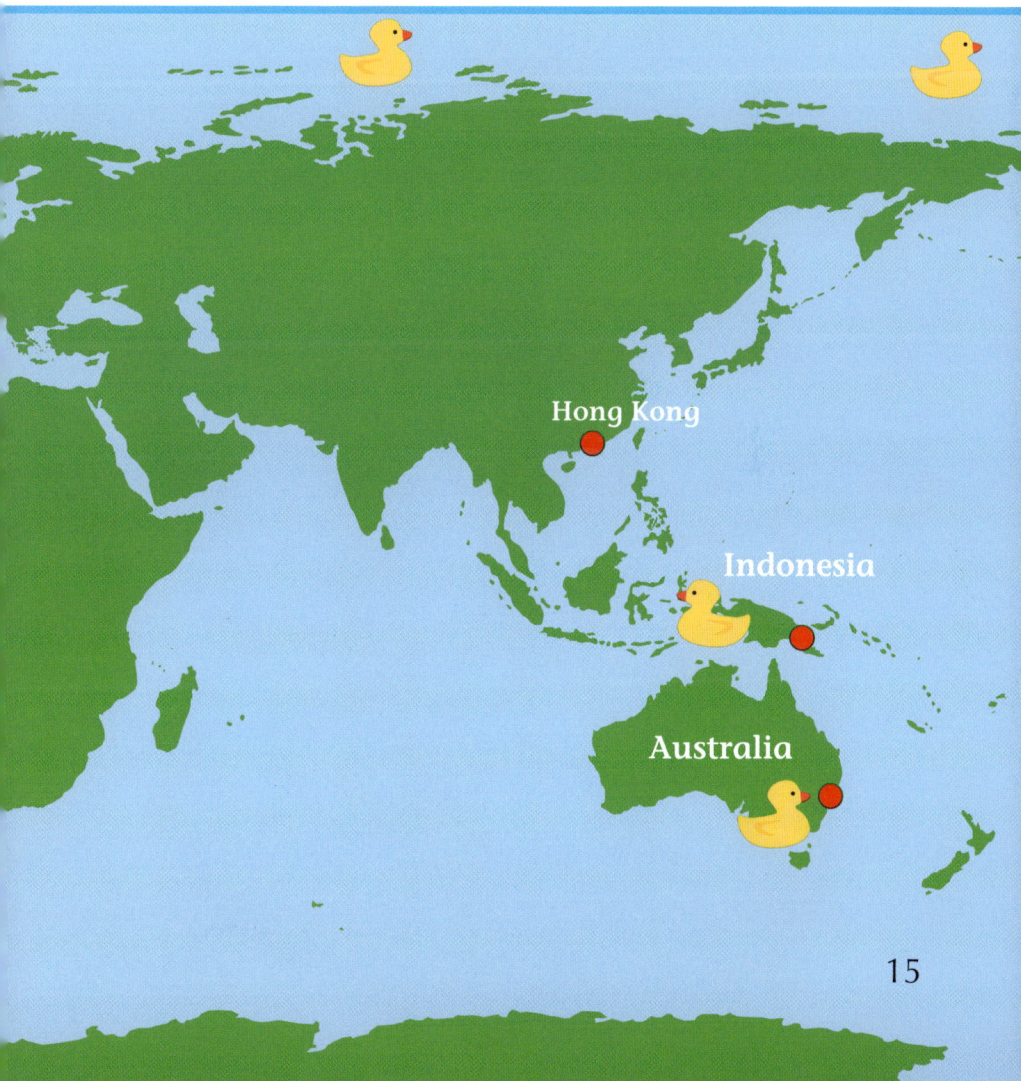

5 Plastic waste

Finding plastic toys on the beach is fun. But plastic **pollution** also damages the planet. Toys washed up on shore show us that plastic drifts for thousands of miles around the world. It can then wash up as waste that harms animals and the environment.

Other drifting plastic, like bottles and shopping bags, breaks down into small pieces called microplastics. Microplastics can be eaten by fish and humans, and this can lead to health problems.

Many people are working to clean up plastic waste on our shores.

Some people hold beach-cleaning days, where everyone joins in to help. Some schools organise these days.

Most people are careful about **recycling** plastic. The world produces over 400 million tonnes of plastic every year. Too much of this plastic ends up as rubbish on our shores.

What could you do to help reduce plastic waste?

Glossary

pilot whales   small, toothed whales

pollution   materials that harm the environment

recycling   making new materials from waste

shipping container   large box to transport goods across oceans

Index

beach 2–3, 6–7, 8–10, 12, 16, 18

bottle 6, 17

container 2, 12–14,

plastic 12–19

sea 8–9, 12, 14

ship 2–6, 12–14

shore 2–5, 15–18

tooth 10–11

toy 12, 14–16

whale 8–9

What washed up?

Natural

whales

tooth

Non-natural

scroll

phones

ship

toys

Ideas for reading

Written by Gill Matthews
Primary Literacy Consultant

Reading objectives:
- be introduced to non-fiction books that are structured in different ways
- discuss and clarify the meanings of words, linking new meanings to known vocabulary
- answer and ask questions

Spoken language objectives:
- articulate and justify answers, arguments and opinions
- give well-structured descriptions, explanations and narratives for different purposes, including for expressing feelings

Curriculum links: Science: Uses of everyday materials; Geography: Geographical skills and fieldwork

Interest words: stranded, damages, drifts

Word count: 729

Resources: litter-picking equipment

Build a context for reading

- Ask children to look at the front cover and to read the title. Discuss what they think the title means. Check whether they are familiar with the phrase *washed up*. Ask why they think the front cover shows a picture of a plastic duck.
- Read the back cover blurb. Ask what they think they are going to find out from reading this book.
- Point out that this is an information book. Discuss the typical features of non-fiction texts that they are familiar with. Give children a few minutes to skim the book to find some of the features they identified.

Understand and apply reading strategies

- Ask children to use the contents page to find the first chapter, which is an introduction to the book.
- Read pp2–3 aloud. Ask children what they think the purpose of an introduction is.